CARLOS ALCARAZ

LUKE HANLON

WWW.APEXEDITIONS.COM

Copyright © 2026 by Apex Editions, Mendota Heights, MN 55120. All rights reserved. No part of this book may be reproduced or utilized in any form or by any means without written permission from the publisher.

Apex is distributed by North Star Editions:
sales@northstareditions.com | 888-417-0195

Produced for Apex by Red Line Editorial.

Photographs ©: Christophe Gateau/picture-alliance/dpa/AP Images, cover, 1; Matthew Stockman/Getty Images Sport/Getty Images, 4–5; Elsa/Getty Images Sport/Getty Images, 6–7; Shutterstock Images, 8–9, 16–17, 18–19, 28–29, 38–39, 58–59; Clive Brunskill/Getty Images Sport/Getty Images, 10–11, 14–15, 24–25, 34–35, 42–43, 46–47, 54–55; Clive Mason/Getty Images Sport/Getty Images, 12–13, 44–45; Buda Mendes/Getty Images Sport/Getty Images, 20–21; Hamish Blair/AP Images, 22–23; Julian Finney/Getty Images Sport/Getty Images, 26–27, 49, 56–57; Frey/TPN/Getty Images Sport/Getty Images, 30–31, 40–41; Sarah Stier/Getty Images Sport/Getty Images, 32–33; Jose Manuel Alvarez/Quality Sport Images/Getty Images Sport/Getty Images, 37; Graham Denholm/Getty Images Sport/Getty Images, 50–51; Quality Sport Images/Getty Images Sport/Getty Images, 52–53

Library of Congress Control Number: 2024951997

ISBN
979-8-89250-719-6 (hardcover)
979-8-89250-771-4 (paperback)
979-8-89250-753-0 (ebook pdf)
979-8-89250-737-0 (hosted ebook)

Printed in the United States of America
Mankato, MN
082025

NOTE TO PARENTS AND EDUCATORS
Apex books are designed to build literacy skills in striving readers. Exciting, high-interest content attracts and holds readers' attention. The text is carefully leveled to allow students to achieve success quickly.

TABLE OF CONTENTS

CHAPTER 1
MAKING HISTORY 4

CHAPTER 2
FATHER AND SON 8

CHAPTER 3
TENNIS STAR 16

CHAPTER 4
ON THE RISE 26

IN THE SPOTLIGHT
BEATING THE BEST 36

CHAPTER 5
MAJOR IMPACT 38

IN THE SPOTLIGHT
INSTANT CLASSIC 48

CHAPTER 6
BEST IN THE WORLD 50

TIMELINE • 58
COMPREHENSION QUESTIONS • 60
GLOSSARY • 62
TO LEARN MORE • 63
ABOUT THE AUTHOR • 63
INDEX • 64

CHAPTER 1

MAKING HISTORY

Carlos Alcaraz was playing in the 2022 US Open final. He smashed a serve. Casper Ruud barely had time to move. The ball zoomed past Ruud for an ace. Alcaraz needed only one more point to win the match.

At the US Open, Carlos Alcaraz blasted serves more than 120 miles per hour (193 km/h).

Ruud scored the next point. Alcaraz responded with a rocket of a serve. Ruud lunged at the ball. But it glanced off his racket and went out of bounds. Alcaraz fell to the ground. He put his hands over his face. At just 19 years old, he had won a major.

BEST IN THE WORLD

After winning the 2022 US Open, Alcaraz became the world No. 1 in men's tennis. He was the youngest men's player ever to earn that ranking. No teenager had been ranked men's No. 1 before.

The US Open is one of four tennis majors. Majors are also known as Grand Slam events.

CHAPTER 2
FATHER AND SON

Carlos Alcaraz Garfia was born on May 5, 2003. He grew up in El Palmar, Spain. His father, Carlos Sr., was a professional tennis player. Carlos Sr. was ranked as one of the best players in Spain.

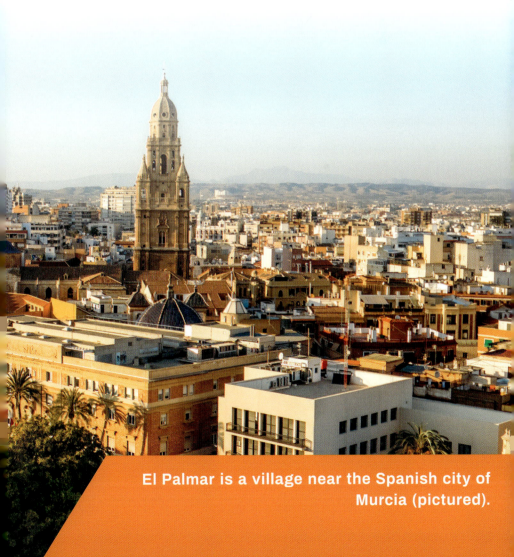

El Palmar is a village near the Spanish city of Murcia (pictured).

Carlos Sr. (far left) became the director of the Real Sociedad Club de Campo after quitting professional tennis.

Carlos Sr.'s career didn't last very long. He didn't make any prize money on tour. So, he stopped playing professional tennis. He decided to coach instead. Carlos Jr. started playing tennis when he was four years old. Carlos Sr. coached his son.

FAMILY CLUB

The Real Sociedad Club de Campo used to be for hunting. But Carlos Jr.'s grandfather built clay tennis courts there. Later, Carlos Jr. learned to play on those clay courts.

Rafael Nadal won his first French Open title in 2005.

When Carlos Jr. was growing up, Rafael Nadal was one of the best tennis players in the world. Nadal was also from Spain. He won 22 majors. Carlos Jr. often watched Nadal's matches. He hoped to be as good as Nadal one day.

JUST LIKE RAFA

Rafael Nadal won the French Open a record 14 times. That tournament is played on clay courts. Like Nadal, Carlos Alcaraz prefers to play on clay. Alcaraz's favorite tournament is also the French Open.

Carlos Jr. grew up with three brothers. They all played tennis.

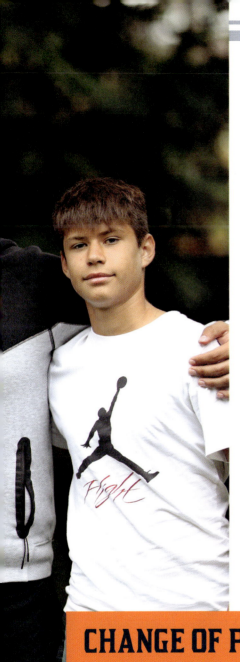

Carlos Jr. was a fast learner. Tennis came easily for him. He had a strong forehand shot. And he could move quickly. That let him cover a lot of ground.

Carlos Jr.'s coaches saw his talent. They thought he could be a champion one day. Carlos Jr. was too good to play against kids his own age. So, the coaches made him play against older kids.

CHANGE OF PLANS

Carlos Jr. was an adaptable player. Sometimes his plan going into a match wouldn't work. So, Carlos Jr. learned to change his playing style on the fly.

CHAPTER 3
TENNIS STAR

Carlos kept practicing. Soon, he needed better coaches. So, he moved to Villena, Spain. Carlos trained at a tennis academy there. Juan Carlos Ferrero became his new coach.

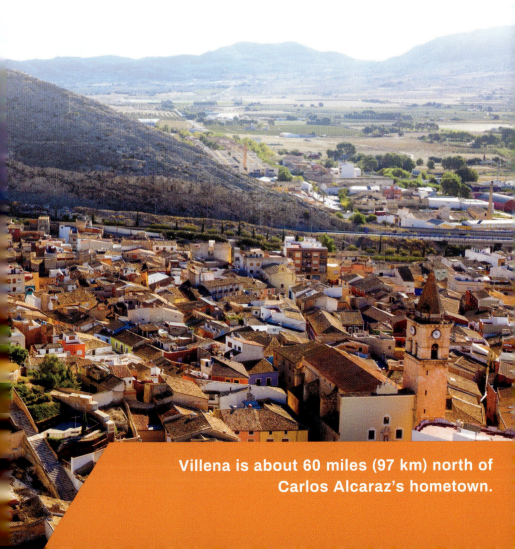

Villena is about 60 miles (97 km) north of Carlos Alcaraz's hometown.

Carlos had lots of success during his junior career. Few players could match his skills. And he could play on any surface. He won most of his matches. With Ferrero's help, Carlos got better and better. He became a professional tennis player in 2018. He was only 15 years old.

TALENTED TEACHER

Juan Carlos Ferrero had a great tennis career. He won the French Open in 2003. He even earned the world No. 1 ranking. Ferrero started coaching after he retired.

Juan Carlos Ferrero played professional tennis for 14 years.

Carlos Alcaraz was 16 years old when he first competed in the Rio Open.

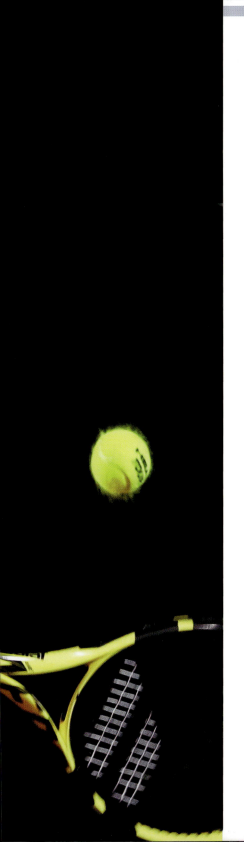

Carlos made it to the top tennis tour in February 2020. His first tournament was the Rio Open in Brazil. Carlos moved around the clay court with ease. He hit hard backhand shots. He used well-timed drop shots, too. Carlos won his first match.

The young player's run ended in the next round. Then, the COVID-19 pandemic shut down the tour. Tennis fans had to wait months to see Carlos play again.

In most tournaments, players must win two sets to take a match. In majors, players must win three sets.

In January and February of 2021, Carlos played in the Australian Open. It was his first time playing in a major. However, the rising star was not afraid to play on a big stage. He won his first match in straight sets.

THE BIG THREE

Starting in the early 2000s, three players dominated men's tennis. They were Roger Federer, Rafael Nadal, and Novak Djokovic. Through 2024, they combined to win 66 majors. All three played their first major at 17 years old. So did Carlos Alcaraz.

Carlos made history in May 2021. He won his first match at the Madrid Open in Spain. He was the youngest player to win a match there. He broke a record set by Rafael Nadal 17 years earlier.

HAPPY BIRTHDAY

A day after his historic win, Carlos Alcaraz faced Rafael Nadal. It was Alcaraz's 18th birthday. Nadal beat him easily. The two players celebrated together after the match, though. The staff brought a birthday cake onto the court for Alcaraz.

Players must win six games to take a set. Nadal beat Alcaraz 6–1 and 6–2 in their two Madrid Open sets.

CHAPTER 4
ON THE RISE

Alcaraz shot up the world rankings. Older players had a hard time dealing with his energy. In June 2021, Alcaraz played in the French Open for the first time. He made it to the third round.

Alcaraz won his match in the second round of the 2021 French Open in straight sets.

Alcaraz played in the Croatia Open in July 2021. Just like the French Open, it had clay courts. Alcaraz won his first four matches. Then he faced Richard Gasquet in the final. Alcaraz showed no nerves in his first final as a pro. His forehand shots zoomed past Gasquet. Alcaraz won in straight sets.

CLAY COURTS

Tennis balls lose speed when they hit clay. Clay also causes unexpected bounces. Alcaraz knew how to handle the courts. He slid over the clay to reach the ball quicker. And he used spin to make his shots hard to hit.

Clay courts can be bumpy and uneven.

Alcaraz had his first run in a major in August 2021. He made it to the third round of the US Open. There, he faced world No. 3 Stefanos Tsitsipas.

The match went to a fifth-set tiebreaker. Alcaraz took a 6–5 lead. Tsitsipas hit a high lob shot. Alcaraz let it bounce. Then he smashed a forehand shot. It was too fast for Tsitsipas. The crowd in New York roared to celebrate Alcaraz's win.

Players must win sets by at least two games. If the set is tied 6–6, they play one last tiebreak game.

Beating Tsitsipas was the biggest win of Alcaraz's career. But the young star's tournament ended in the quarterfinals. Alcaraz hurt his right leg. The injury was too painful to play through. Alcaraz had to quit during the second set.

HARD HITTER

Alcaraz showed his strength at the US Open. In the third round, he hit a serve 134 miles per hour (216 km/h). Tsitsipas said he'd never seen anyone hit that hard.

Alcaraz was the youngest men's player since 1989 to reach the fourth round of the US Open.

In March 2022, Alcaraz played Rafael Nadal for the second time. Nadal won again. The two soon faced off for a third time. In May, they played in the Madrid Open. Alcaraz beat his hero this time. But he wasn't finished. Alcaraz made it all the way to the final.

TOUGH COMPETITION

Before the 2022 Madrid Open, Nadal was ranked No. 3 in the world. Alcaraz beat him in the quarterfinals. No. 1 Novak Djokovic waited for Alcaraz in the semifinals. Many tennis fans think Djokovic is the best player ever. But Alcaraz beat Djokovic in a third-set tiebreaker.

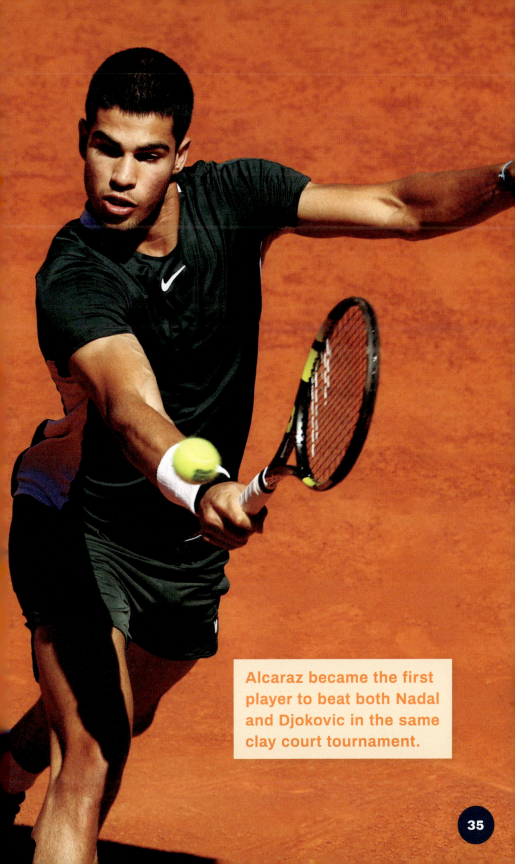

Alcaraz became the first player to beat both Nadal and Djokovic in the same clay court tournament.

IN THE SPOTLIGHT

BEATING THE BEST

Carlos Alcaraz faced No. 2 Alexander Zverev in the 2022 Madrid Open final. Alcaraz kept Zverev off-balance. He hit drop shots with lots of backspin. The shots were difficult to return. Alcaraz won the match.

At 19, Alcaraz was the youngest Madrid Open champion ever. And he had beat three great players on the way. The win gave Alcaraz the No. 6 ranking. He was quickly becoming one of the world's best players.

ALCARAZ WON THE 2022 MADRID OPEN FINAL IN STRAIGHT SETS.

CHAPTER 5

MAJOR IMPACT

Some fans thought Alcaraz could win his first major at the 2022 French Open. Alcaraz made it through the first four rounds. But Alexander Zverev ended the young star's run in the quarterfinals.

Alcaraz took Alexander Zverev to a fourth-set tiebreaker in the 2022 French Open.

Next, Alcaraz made it to the 2022 Wimbledon quarterfinals. He lost to Jannik Sinner. The two met again at the US Open quarterfinals. This time, Alcaraz won. He won in the semifinals, too. Those two matches were long. But Alcaraz still had energy for the final. He beat Casper Ruud to win his first major and earn the No. 1 ranking.

MARATHON MATCH

In the US Open quarterfinals, Alcaraz saved a match point in the fourth set. Then he won in the fifth set. The match ended at 2:50 a.m. No match in US Open history had ever ended that late.

Alcaraz's quarterfinals match at the 2022 US Open lasted 5 hours and 15 minutes.

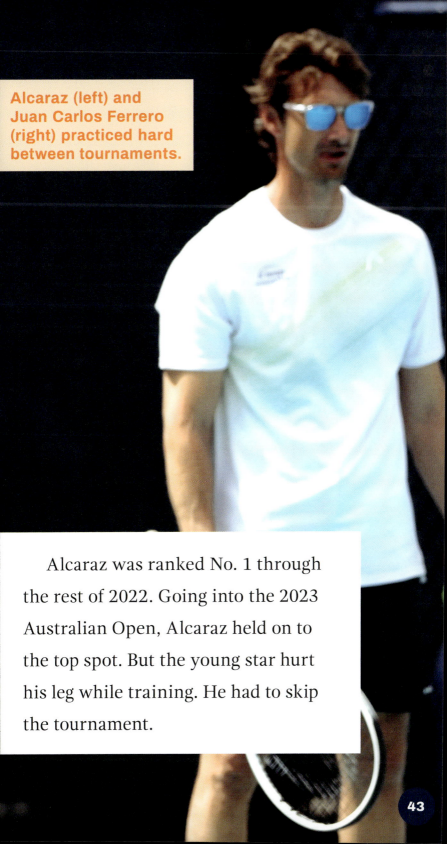

Alcaraz (left) and Juan Carlos Ferrero (right) practiced hard between tournaments.

Alcaraz was ranked No. 1 through the rest of 2022. Going into the 2023 Australian Open, Alcaraz held on to the top spot. But the young star hurt his leg while training. He had to skip the tournament.

Alcaraz was healthy for the 2023 French Open. He faced Novak Djokovic in the semifinals. Alcaraz won a tight second set. That tied the match. But his right hand began to cramp in the third set. Later in the match, he got cramps in his legs. Djokovic easily won the next two sets.

TOO NERVOUS

Alcaraz was nervous to play Djokovic. Alcaraz had beaten him before. But playing against Djokovic in a major was different. Alcaraz said the nerves led to his cramps.

Novak Djokovic hit shots all over the court. Alcaraz had trouble chasing them down.

Alcaraz got over the loss quickly. He moved on to the 2023 Queen's Club Championships in England. Like Wimbledon, Queen's is played on grass. Alcaraz won the tournament. It was his first tournament win on grass.

GRASS COURTS

Playing on grass is different from playing on clay. Players can't slide on grass courts. Also, tennis balls don't lose as much speed. Alcaraz had to use a different playing style. He won matches with quick footwork and strong shots.

Alcaraz beat Alex de Minaur in straight sets to win the 2023 Queen's Club final.

IN THE SPOTLIGHT

INSTANT CLASSIC

Six weeks after the French Open semifinals, Alcaraz met Novak Djokovic again. This time, they faced off in the 2023 Wimbledon final. Djokovic had won the tournament four times in a row.

Alcaraz and Djokovic rocketed powerful shots back and forth. They played for 4 hours and 42 minutes. It was the third-longest final in Wimbledon history. Finally, Alcaraz hit a perfectly placed shot to the corner of the court. Djokovic couldn't return it. Alcaraz won his first Wimbledon title.

ALCARAZ WAS ONLY 20 YEARS OLD DURING THE 2023 WIMBLEDON TOURNAMENT.

CHAPTER 6

BEST IN THE WORLD

Alcaraz lost in the semifinals of the 2023 US Open. Then he was outplayed in the quarterfinals of the 2024 Australian Open. His run at the 2024 French Open looked like it would end before the final, too.

In the 2024 Australian Open quarterfinals, Alexander Zverev beat Alcaraz in four sets.

Alcaraz played Jannik Sinner in the French Open semifinals. Sinner won two of the first three sets. But Alcaraz stormed back. He won the last two sets. Next, he faced Alexander Zverev in the final. Alcaraz fell behind two sets to one. However, he got better as the match went on. He came back to win his first French Open.

COURT MASTER

Alcaraz won the US Open in 2022. That tournament is on a hard court. Then he won Wimbledon in 2023. That tournament is on grass. The 2024 French Open win gave him a major on clay, too.

Alcaraz was the youngest men's player to win a major on all three court surfaces.

The comeback wins at the French Open were nothing new for Alcaraz. He always seemed to play better late in matches. Alcaraz wasn't afraid to take risky shots in big moments.

In the 2024 Wimbledon final, Alcaraz faced Novak Djokovic again. In 2023, it had taken five sets for Alcaraz to win. This time, Alcaraz won the final in three sets.

Alcaraz's wins put him at 4–0 in major finals. Only Roger Federer had done that before.

Alcaraz (bottom) and Nadal (top) won their first two Olympic matches in straight sets.

Next, Alcaraz played at the 2024 Paris Olympics. He faced Djokovic for the gold medal. The first two sets both went to tiebreakers. Djokovic took them both to win gold. The match was another classic between the two great rivals.

DREAM PARTNER

Alcaraz also played doubles at the Olympics. His partner was Rafael Nadal. The duo lost in the quarterfinals. But Alcaraz said it was a dream come true to play with Nadal.

TIMELINE

2003 — Carlos Alcaraz Garfia is born on May 5 in El Palmar, Spain.

2020 — Carlos plays his first match on the top professional tennis tour.

2021 — At 17, Carlos appears in his first major and wins in the first round of the Australian Open.

2022 — On May 6, Alcaraz beats his childhood idol, Rafael Nadal, for the first time.

2022
On September 11, Alcaraz wins his first major tournament, the US Open.

2023
Alcaraz defeats Novak Djokovic for his first Wimbledon title.

2024
Alcaraz wins the French Open on June 9. He becomes the youngest player to win a major on all three court surfaces.

2024
On July 14, Alcaraz wins his second straight Wimbledon title.

COMPREHENSION QUESTIONS

Write your answers on a separate piece of paper.

1. Write a paragraph that explains the main ideas of Chapter 5.

2. What skills do you think make Carlos Alcaraz a great tennis player? Why?

3. Which surface is Alcaraz's favorite to play on?
    - A. a clay court
    - B. a grass court
    - C. a hard court

4. Why were the 2024 Olympics special for Alcaraz?
    - A. He got to team up with his childhood hero.
    - B. He played against Novak Djokovic for the first time.
    - C. He won a gold medal.

5. What does **adaptable** mean in this book?

*Carlos Jr. was an **adaptable** player. Sometimes his plan going into a match wouldn't work. So, Carlos Jr. learned to change his playing style on the fly.*

    A. not able to change
    B. able to quickly make a new plan
    C. always using the same plan

6. What does **comeback** mean in this book?

*The **comeback** wins at the French Open were nothing new for Alcaraz. He always seemed to play better late in matches.*

    A. taking the lead right away but losing it
    B. taking the lead near the end after being behind
    C. playing the same way the whole time

Answer key on page 64.

GLOSSARY

academy
A place where young athletes train for a specific sport.

ace
A serve that the returning player doesn't touch, earning a point for the server.

dominated
Played better than others and won often.

drop shots
Shots that are hit just over the net, forcing opponents to run forward.

lob shot
A shot hit high into the air and deep into the opponent's side of the court.

match point
When a player has a chance to win the match by winning the next point.

professional
Having to do with people who get paid for what they do.

rivals
Players who have an intense competition against one another.

straight sets
When a player wins all of the sets in a match.

tiebreaker
A way to decide a set if both players win six games. To win a tiebreaker, a player must reach seven points and win by at least two points.

TO LEARN MORE

BOOKS

Blue, Tyler. *Stars of World Tennis*. Abbeville Kids, 2024.

Goldstein, Margaret J. *Meet Novak Djokovic: Tennis Superstar*. Lerner Publications, 2025.

Price, Karen. *GOATs of Tennis*. Abdo Publishing, 2022.

ONLINE RESOURCES

Visit **www.apexeditions.com** to find links and resources related to this title.

ABOUT THE AUTHOR

Luke Hanlon is a sportswriter and editor based in Minneapolis. He's written dozens of nonfiction sports books for kids and spends a lot of his free time watching his favorite Minnesota sports teams.

INDEX

Alcaraz, Carlos, Sr., 9, 11
Australian Open, 23, 43, 50

clay, 11, 13, 21, 28, 47, 52
Croatia Open, 28

Djokovic, Novak, 23, 34, 44, 48, 54, 57

El Palmar, Spain, 9

Federer, Roger, 23
Ferrero, Juan Carlos, 17–18
French Open, 13, 18, 26, 28, 38, 44, 48, 50, 52, 54

Gasquet, Richard, 28
grass, 46–47, 52

Madrid Open, 24, 34, 36

Nadal, Rafael, 13, 23–24, 34, 57

Olympics, 57

Queen's Club Championships, 46

Real Sociedad Club de Campo, 11
Rio Open, 21
Ruud, Casper, 4, 6, 40

Sinner, Jannik, 40, 52

Tsitsipas, Stefanos, 30, 32

US Open, 4, 6, 30, 32, 40, 50, 52

Villena, Spain, 17

Wimbledon, 40, 46, 48, 52, 54

Zverev, Alexander, 36, 38, 52

ANSWER KEY:
1. Answers will vary; 2. Answers will vary; 3. A; 4. A; 5. B; 6.